by

Phillip A. Ketron, MBA, CSA, NCG

Contents

Foreword

Let me start by stating that I am not an attorney, accountant, or a Social Security or Veteran's Administration expert, and I encourage you to seek professional guidance for specific questions related to the topics discussed in this book. This book is designed to provide insight and invoke thought into some of the issues that I have come across while serving as a conservator, power of attorney, trustee, executor, and health care surrogate. All of the names of my clients have been changed.

If you have similar experiences that are discussed in this book that you feel would benefit readers, please send them to me at pketron@srcareconsulting.com. After all, most people will only experience death and dying of a loved one a few times in their life. There is no learning curve and plenty of heart-wrenching mistakes can tear a family apart.

Death is a subject matter that people don't readily embrace or discuss, so I have thrown in a joke or two along the way to lighten the mood. After all, there is a 100 percent probability of dying. The question is whether you will kill your family in the process.

Introduction

I've sure gotten old!

I've had two bypass surgeries, a hip replacement,

new knees, fought prostate cancer and diabetes,

I'm half blind,

can't hear anything quieter than a jet engine,

take 40 different medications that

make me dizzy, winded, and subject to blackouts.

Have bouts with dementia.

Have poor circulation;

hardly feel my hands and feet anymore.

Can't remember if I'm 85 or 92.

Have lost all my friends.

But, I thank God every day that I still have my driver's license.

Author Unknown

* * *

If you are like most people, we all poke fun at old age, but at the same time, we dread it. Personally, I would like to die in my sleep after having a great day with my family. I don't want extended illness, long-term care, nursing home, diapers . . . you name it. I especially don't want to be a burden on my family financially or otherwise. What I do want is to be in control and not have my family torn apart over what I leave behind, assuming that there is anything left.

You don't have to look too far to see families that are struggling with taking care of the needs of an ailing parent/spouse. Extended illness can wipe out a family from both a mental and/or financial standpoint. Mistakes will happen, followed by the "blame game." No family is immune.

Today's family looks quite different than it did thirty or more years ago. Over half the families now are blended families. Some families have half-siblings, while others have stepchildren or a combination of both. Having at least one step-grandchild is the norm for seniors, not the exception. This all leads to complexity and the potential for conflict at the death of a parent or stepparent.

Even families with biological children are at risk to potential conflicts at the death of a parent. I experienced firsthand family conflict of a man padlocking the doors to his mother's house after she died. No one was going to enter his mother's house without his approval or knowledge. You would have thought his mother was wealthy and had many valuable assets, but in reality, most of her belongings were eventually donated to charitable organizations or thrown away.

The good news is that many of the burdens can be reduced or eliminated through some simple education and planning on your part—putting you in the driver seat, so to speak. There is no learning curve, as you will only die once. So, keep your driver's license and let's embark on a road trip that is, unfortunately, a dead end.

Chapter 1: Family Favors

Question:

Why are seniors so slow to clean out the basement, attic, or garage?

Answer:

They know that as soon as they do, one of their adult kids will want to store stuff there.

Author Unknown

* * *

Forrest was a Korean War veteran who had allowed his only daughter and her children to move in with him after his wife died. Forrest made the daughter his power of attorney (POA) so that she could take care of his financial and health care needs. Most would say that it was a win-win situation with his daughter providing support and Forrest providing a place to stay for the single-parent daughter and her children.

Not long after the daughter moved in, she began to neglect Forrest's basic needs. She used Forrest's money for her needs and relegated him to his room. After a couple of months, Forrest ended up in the emergency room malnourished and in poor health resulting in a multiple-day inpatient admission. Adult Protective Services got involved and they would not allow Forrest to return to the home with the daughter still living there. I'm still not sure why the daughter wasn't charged with abuse or neglect, but she wasn't.

Forrest knew his daughter and grandchildren didn't have a place to live if he kicked them out, so he sought housing elsewhere. With assistance from a woman at an assisted-living facility, he applied and received a veteran's benefit called "Aid and Attendance." This resource-based benefit is only available to veterans who served during a war or police action. The benefit is also available for spouses of qualifying veterans.

The Aid and Attendance benefit included a back payment from the original application date. Combined with his retirement check and social security, Forrest had plenty of money to cover his bills; however, his first check to the assisted-living facility bounced. This is when I was asked to get involved.

During the transition from home, to hospital, to assisted living, Forrest hadn't revoked the power of attorney (POA) he had granted his daughter. She used the POA to buy a cell phone, subscribe to DIRECTV, etc., all using *his* credit information. She also used the POA to raid his bank account and withdraw everything from his safety deposit box including US Savings bonds that he had set aside to pay for his funeral expenses. While I don't have proof, I am pretty sure you can guess what the daughter did with the savings bonds.

Once discovered, Forrest revoked the POA and we contacted the local police department and filed a complaint. Since a POA is a contract, we were limited to civil actions against the daughter, as the monetary amounts didn't warrant criminal charges based upon the statutes of the state of Tennessee. Realizing that the daughter did not have the means to repay any monetary damages if awarded, we didn't take any legal action.

I recommended that we had the daughter evicted from the house and put it up for sale. My concern was primarily for Forrest's wellbeing, as his health was declining. I knew there might come a day when he could no longer stay in the assisted-living facility and would have to either sell the house or have a lien placed against it. Forrest was adamant that his daughter and grandchildren could stay there until someone forced them to move out of the house.

After the revocation of the POA, Forrest's daughter had little to do with him. She changed the locks to the house and wouldn't let him back in to retrieve some of his possessions. Still, Forrest refused to take any action to remove his daughter and grandchildren. Looking back, I think he knew he didn't have long to live, and he didn't want this to be the lasting memory of his only child and grandchildren.

When Forrest died, the only known life insurance policy had a loan balance that left little money for his final expenses. The funeral home called the daughter multiple times in attempts to get her to make and take financial responsibility for her father's funeral arrangements. The body had been at the funeral home so long that the funeral home had to proceed with final disposition of the body regardless of payment. Later, I discovered that she was the sole beneficiary to a life policy that was part of Forrest's retirement that she didn't want the funeral home or other creditors to know about. I couldn't believe someone would disrespect their father's body after all he had done and given to her, but it happens every day.

Takeaways

The title of this book, *How to Die . . . Without Killing Your Family,* may be confusing based upon Forrest's story. This real-life example was used to illustrate that there isn't a foolproof happy-ending approach to dying in which your family will be in complete harmony singing "Kumbaya" at your funeral. Family members have issues that have nothing to do with you, and they will continue to have issues after you have passed. That being said, there are still some things that can be learned from Forrest.

First, a power of attorney (POA) is a powerful document and comes in many forms. For our purposes, the two most common are general durable (aka financial) and "health care." The financial POA, unless limited, allows the POA to buy, sell, transact, etc. any financial transaction as if they were you. The health care POA allows your POA to make decisions as it relates to your medical treatment.

You can have more than one person named as your POA, but this can cause problems if your POAs disagree, such as with a health care decision. Naming more than one financial POA increases the potential for exploitation. Most attorneys will tell you not to grant a POA to anyone to whom you cannot trust, and I agree. But what do you if you don't have anyone?

My recommendation is to have two separate POA documents—one for financial, and one for health care—and to not have the two documents combined. The financial POA is the most dangerous document as far as exploitation goes and should be "springing." This adds the requirement of a physician's statement that you are no longer able to make decisions on your own before being valid.

Since medical emergencies can happen without warning and decisions will need to be made, the health care POA should be immediate, not springing. The health care POA is so specific in scope that there is little opportunity for misuse. Combined with an advanced medical directive that will be discussed in Chapter 2: Dying Wishes, you can be in complete control of any medical decision.

Second, your financial assets determine who, what, when, where, and how as it relates to your health care. The more money you have, the more options. Most seniors want to live in their own home and not in an assisted-living facility or nursing home. This is all possible provided that you have long-term care insurance, retirement assets, etc. to pay for cost of care that can run $12,000 a month or higher.

According to a 2010 MetLife study, *Broken Trust: Elders, Family and Finances,* family members rank second when it comes to victimizing a senior. In reality, family members may actually be the top instigators as seniors are less likely to report/prosecute family such as with Forrest. If you become a victim of financial exploitation, you may only get a portion of your money back. Once it is gone, it is gone, which may take away some of your health care options as well.

Third, I feel that every family needs a safety deposit box as a central location for all important documents, jewelry, etc. This will keep your family members from having to search all over the house for these documents. Did you know that there are over $1 billion in unclaimed life insurance policies, investments, and other personal property? Don't let yours be added to the growing list.

Forrest's example does show a weakness in having a safety deposit box, as it can be cleaned out, just like your assets at home. I wish there was a simple solution, but there isn't. One approach would be to "conveniently" lose the key after all the important documents have been placed in the box. This would require the key to be drilled, which would make it harder for someone to just help themselves to your stuff. If anything, at least you would have documentation as to who has accessed your box.

Finally, it is best to have your funeral arrangement prepaid and not rely on a life insurance policy or other assets to pay for your final expenses. As with Forrest, these instruments can be changed, altered, redeemed, or go missing resulting in your not having any money to pay funeral expenses. Your assets may also get depleted paying for your health care; however, you should note that prepaying funeral expenses is an allowable spend-down expense if you're trying to qualify for government assistance.

One of the hardest parts of my job is dealing with the body of a client after death when there are no financial assets to pay for the final disposition. The lowest cost alternative is cremation, which runs at least $2,500. A bare-bones burial will cost twice as much.

The last gift that you should give your family is to take care of all funeral arrangements from the casket, headstone, etc. This will allow your family time to grieve, reflect, and celebrate your life versus creating the opportunity for your family to overspend and disagree on what you would have wanted. Do your family a favor and take care of your pre-need arrangement today.

Chapter 2: Dying Wishes

I received a call from an attorney who wanted to know if I would be willing to serve as a conservator for Bernie, who was on a ventilator in the Intensive Care Unit of a local hospital. A conservator, referred to as a guardian in some states, is a court-appointed person who is authorized to make both financial and health care decisions for someone who can't do so for themselves. A conservator is similar to a POA but is awarded through a court, not by a local attorney.

Bernie was disabled and had an accident at his home. He had been on the ventilator at one hospital, then transferred to another hospital that specialized in removing patients from a ventilator. Unfortunately, the procedure was unsuccessful. He was not responding to treatment and had no brain activity when he was transferred to the second hospital. All of this occurred over a period of four months.

My first question was whether Bernie had any family members. Bernie did have family members, but there were some problems. Apparently, Bernie's mother had a terminal illness and ended up dying after Bernie's initial admission. She asked her daughter to do all that she could for Bernie. The daughter in turn wanted full treatment for Bernie and would not make any health decisions to the contrary regardless of the recommendations of the health professionals. She was trying to fulfill her dying mother's wishes in the best way she knew how. Bernie, on the other hand, was dying a slow and possibly painful death.

An emergency court session was held, and I was appointed as Bernie's conservator. The sister broke down in tears and had to be transported to the emergency room for treatment. I felt sorry for the sister, as she was put in a very difficult position. I also was put into a difficult situation.

Part of serving as a conservator is having to make decisions regarding medical treatment. This includes whether or not someone is to be placed on or removed from a ventilator, whether to provide nutrition, such as through a feeding tube, etc. In a perfect world, I would have had time to get to know my client, or at least have had an advanced medical directive to follow in such cases. Unfortunately, I had neither.

I met with the physician and talked with the nursing staff and others who were involved with Bernie's care. There was a consensus that Bernie was dying and other surgeries would simply delay the inevitable, not to mention being potentially painful due to the removal of dead skin. This was one of the most difficult decisions I have ever made in my life. What would I do if Bernie were my brother? What would I want done if I was in the same situation as Bernie?

I lost a lot of sleep over the next couple of days, requested prayer for wisdom, and prayed continuously. I eventually made the decision to remove Bernie from the ventilator and he died shortly thereafter. Even though he wasn't a family member, the decision will forever be entrenched in my life. I encourage others to take steps to prevent a stranger, such as me, from making their life-ending decision.

Takeaways

When you are dying, one of the worst things you can do to a spouse, child, or other family member is to have them make what is referred to as a "death-bed promise." These promises are usually vague, such as, "Promise me you will take care of your mother," or "Promise me that you will never put your father in a nursing home," etc. Your family members are going to grieve your passing, and this type of promise can add guilt to the grief if they are unable to fulfill your wishes. This can lead to some disastrous results, as was the case with Bernie.

The sister was grieving her mother's passing and then she had to deal with a dying brother, Bernie. I believe that the grief and her inability to take care of her brother were too much for her to handle. Deep down, she was probably relieved to no longer have to make medical decisions for her brother. All of this could have been avoided had Bernie prepared an advanced medical directive prior to his illness. Even if contrary to her mother's wishes, it would have given the sister peace in knowing that Bernie's medical directives were being followed.

An advanced medical directive (AMD) is an extension of the health care POA discussed in Chapter 1: Family Favors and comes in many forms. In its basic form, an AMD establishes whether you want to be resuscitated, placed on a ventilator, receive a feeding tube, etc. Most health care providers are going to ask whether you have one or if you would like to prepare one prior to treatment.

No single form is going to cover every situation, so it is paramount to have conversations with your health care POA. You should be specific as to when you want CPR, life support/artificial support, etc. The most difficult of which is the withholding of food and water. No health professional will deny these basic needs if you ask and are able to absorb them;

however, if you are unable to ask for them, a decision will need to be made as to whether a feeding tube will need to be used. When you get to this point, it may be in your best interest to have these withheld, which should be your choice, not your health care POA's choice.

Whether you do anything else for your family, preparing an advanced medical directive should be at the top of your list. It is a very simple document, and you can add wording to the form so your health care POA and family know exactly what you want and don't want. Personally, I encourage my clients to complete an AMD called "5 Wishes." This AMD was developed by the Aging With Dignity organization and is available as a free download from their website at www.agingwithdignity.org. This document has saved me many nights of lost sleep and provided peace that I was doing *exactly* what my client wanted me to do.

Chapter 3: Care Giving Dilemma

Tim and Karen Reynolds had two sons and two daughters, all of who lived locally. Their adult children had families of their own and many responsibilities. Tim had hearing problems but was in pretty good shape. Tim loved working outdoors and especially working in the garden. The children would often joke that Tim liked being outdoors to get a little break from his wife, Karen, who liked to talk. They also joked that his hearing wasn't really that bad; he just had the ability to tune Karen out.

Karen had fibromyalgia, arthritis, and sinus problems necessitating frequent medical office visits. In some ways, Karen was a hypochondriac who would schedule a doctor's appointment just in case she needed it. I am being a little facetious, but I do think she enjoyed the social interaction. She loved to sit in waiting rooms and talk to those around her to compare notes on doctors. If she didn't like the doctor, she was more than happy to tell you that as well. Did I mention that she liked to talk!

Due to Karen's medical problems, she didn't drive, so Tim would take her to doctor appointments. They had their little routine until Tim had an accident, resulting in an open wound fracture to his leg. The oldest son, Tim Jr. (Junior), was retired, so he volunteered to take his dad to his follow-up medical appointments. Tim's leg wasn't healing very well, and this led to even more treatments. Soon, Karen began asking Junior to take her to the doctor as well. Junior didn't realize how many appointments his mom actually had until he started taking her.

To compensate Junior for his time, his parents would often take him out to eat before or after the office visit. They even offered Junior money for gas, his time, etc., but he declined at first. After all, it was his parents and he had a sense of obligation. The other children would try to help, but with their own families and full-time jobs, they simply couldn't.

Junior, being the oldest, started taking more control of his parents' affairs. His name was added to his parents' checking account so he could write checks on their behalf. Junior soon began to reimburse himself for gas and other out-of-pocket expenses that he had incurred while taking care of his parents. To my knowledge, he never charged a dime for all the time he'd spent taking them to the doctor, paying their bills, etc.

One day, Karen's daughter took her to a medical appointment, and as was common, she asked to treat her daughter to lunch. They went to lunch, but the daughter paid for her own meal, knowing that her parents had meager means. She started to question whether they paid for Junior's meals and the response was "all the time." The daughter then became more concerned when she learned that Junior's name had been added to her parents' banking accounts. She contacted her other siblings, worried about what had been going on.

When questioned, Junior's response would be what you would anticipate. "Fine," he said, "I will just let the rest of you take care of Mom and Dad." Junior was upset and I can't say that I blame him. Because of all the family turmoil, they hired me to start assisting with their parents.

I charge for my time and there would now be the additional expense to hire care givers to take Tim and Karen to their medical appointments. This seemed contradictory to me, as Junior hadn't charged them a dime. Junior only started reimbursing himself for normal expenses after the price of gas had gotten so high and it seemed that he was constantly driving back and forth to appointments. His only form of compensation was to be treated to a meal.

Junior's siblings jumped in with their accusations before looking at the big picture. Junior was actually doing his parents and them a favor, but it was too late now. What this was really about was control. The other siblings simply did not trust that Junior was doing the right thing. They formulated their opinions over paying for meals. Really?

As far as I know, Junior is not speaking to his siblings to this day, as his feelings were hurt. "How dare they accuse me of doing something wrong after all I've done while they were working and attending to their own needs. It will be a cold day in hell before I ever help again," he informed me. Sounds silly, but it happens in a lot of families.

Takeaways

Care giving is hard work. Tending to one parent's needs is difficult. Tending to both can be almost impossible. There is a good chance that you will have to care for one or more of your parents. When one parent dies, loneliness can set in, resulting in your not only having to be a care giver but a surrogate companion.

In the example above, Tim Sr. was fairly easy to accommodate. Karen, on the other hand, was labor-intensive.

Her high demand for medical services compiled with her personality could wear down most anyone. Ironically, Junior was doing a great job of taking care of his parents, and I can't say that I blame him for being upset when wrongly accused.

This brings up an issue that needs to be addressed. Should your children receive some form of compensation when and if they are required to provide assistance? In a perfect world, all four children would have shared in the care giving responsibilities. By doing so, it would have placed an equal burden on each, but this isn't reality.

In the example above, all of the children lived local, but this is rarely the case. For example, my sister lives in Florida with her husband and her two children, and she is the principal of a high school. It's not that she wouldn't want to help with our parents; it's just not feasible unless she would be willing to quit her job and move seven hundred miles away. Our parents wouldn't want this type of sacrifice on her part, as I am sure you wouldn't for your children in similar situations.

In most families, the daughter(s) are the primary care givers. If the child is in the medical profession, it is almost a guarantee. Men sometimes get off a little easier, when in reality we can do pretty much anything the daughter can do.

When possible, I think it is best for sons to take care of their father and daughters to take care of their mother.

Another word of caution is for those who have a child named after their father, whether it is Junior, Senior, or so forth. Make sure that Sr., Jr., III, etc. is clearly detailed on the check. It is an absolute nightmare when it doesn't and can cause problems when reporting to the Internal Revenue Service.

Chapter 4: Going, Going, Going . . . Gone

THE SENILITY PRAYER:

Grant me the senility to forget the people I never liked anyway, the good fortune to run into the ones I do, and the eyesight to tell the difference.

Author Unknown

* * *

Are you prepared for the high cost of long-term care? Henry and Louis Jones were not. Henry and Louis were the typical middle-class family. Henry was diagnosed with Alzheimer's disease and the family knew there would come a day when it was no longer safe for him to remain in the home.

Louis was relatively healthy. She was smaller in stature compared to Henry, so she was limited in her ability to take care of her husband. They had two children, one daughter who lived close by, and a son who lived over 150 miles away. The only assets Henry and Louis had were there home, which was valued around $300,000, and an individual retirement account (IRA) plan worth approximately $250,000.

Henry and Louis had a combined social security benefit of around $2,300 per month, which was supplemented by a monthly withdraw from their IRA of around $1,700 a month. While they didn't have a house payment, they had a lot of expenses, especially for prescription drugs, as Henry would typically hit what is referred to as the Medicare Part D "doughnut hole" within the first five months of the year. While in the doughnut hole, Henry could easily spend $800–$1,000 just on prescription drugs.

The daughter had a full-time job and was doing the best she could to help while at the same time meeting the needs of her own family. Louis was becoming more and more exhausted trying to take care of Henry, so they decided to get help from a non-medical agency. Their standard contract required a minimum of four hours per visit at a cost of $18.50 per hour. This at least allowed Louis to get out of the house to buy groceries, get her hair done, etc. In reality, it was worth the money just to give Louis a break. The cost for this care was around $350 per month.

As Henry's disease progressed, they needed more and more care, and they eventually had a non-medical caregiver come by five days a week with the daughter helping on the weekends. The cost of this care grew to approximately $1,600 a month. This required increasing their monthly withdraw from the IRA.

Twenty percent of those diagnosed with Alzheimer's disease get what is referred to as the "sundown syndrome." This syndrome results in poor sleep patterns and agitation as the sun goes down. Henry developed the sundown syndrome and began to wander through the house at night, resulting in even more stress on Louis. The cost to have someone stay the night seven days a week was not affordable at approximate cost of $4,500 a month.

The family's first thought was to find someone less expensive than what the agency was charging. They asked around, talked to friends, posted an ad in the newspaper, Craigslist, etc., but finding reliable care givers was tough. Long story short, the care givers hired proved unreliable, and concerns mounted over some of their trustworthiness as items started to become missing from the home.

The son was adamantly opposed to the suggestion of placing Henry in an assisted-living facility and especially not a nursing home—that is until he spent the night at their home. He saw firsthand the amount of work and stress it was to provide care for his father. To have twenty-four-hour care seven days a week would cost his parents $7,300 per month at $10 per hour to as high as $13,500 a month at $18.50 per hour using an agency. This was simply not doable.

The family then looked at other options, and the decision was made to place Henry in a secure unit of an assisted-living facility at a cost of $4,500 per month. This cost was based upon the level of care that he required and didn't include Henry's prescription drug costs, which had continued to increase. Combined with Louis staying in their home, the Jones's monthly expenditures had now grown to over $7,000 a month.

The son and daughter soon began to play the "what-if" game. What if Dad has to go into a nursing home? What if the nursing home wants the house as collateral for payment? This led to the son and daughter talking their mother into signing over the house to them via a quit claim deed. They couldn't imagine how their mother and father could have worked all their lives to have it all spent away on long-term expenses.

Several months later, Henry did in fact have to go to a nursing home. People don't die from Alzheimer's but from an associated illness. When Henry was diagnosed with kidney disease, his level of care exceeded the level that could be managed in the assisted living, so a nursing home was his only choice at a cost of over $6,000 per month. By the time Henry died, their resources had been greatly diminished, leaving questions as to how they would take care of Louis in her time of need. All of Henry and Louis's life savings was pretty much gone.

Takeaways

Did you know that how much money you have determines who, what, when, where, and how you receive medical treatment? The more money you have, the more choices are available. For example, you can get twenty-four-hour, seven-days-a-week care in your home . . . as long as you have the money. If you run out, then you will be limited to facilities that take government subsidized care.

My wife used to work with someone who stated that when she became old and chronically ill, it would be cheaper to buy a perpetual ticket on a cruise line than to stay at a nursing home. At least on a cruise ship there is room service, entertainment, and you can get a little sunshine. Sounds like a great idea to me!

Most people don't realize just how expensive long-term care can be and don't plan for these expenditures. If you are under age eighty and in relatively good health, you may still be able to buy long-term care insurance or one of the hybrid life insurance or annuities with a long-term care rider. If you are older than eighty or in bad health, I hope you have accumulated enough money to pay for these expenses, because your only option will be to pay from your personal funds as you will be declined for coverage.

The biggest objection to buying long-term care insurance is the cost which can run several hundred dollars a month. Granted, the cost of this type of coverage isn't cheap, but would you rather pay several hundred dollars each month or the $4,000–$7,000 each month in long-term care expenses.

Another objection is that you don't want to waste the money should you die and not having used it. You pretty much do the same thing with your homeowners and car insurance every day, but when you have a claim, you sure are glad you have the coverage.

One way to think about long-term care insurance is that you are insuring the assets you have spent a lifetime accruing. The two biggest fears that a senior has beyond their health is being alone and outliving their money. Long-term care insurance can take care of both, as it will protect your money. And if you have money, I am sure someone out there is looking for a sugar daddy or momma, which will take care of your loneliness.

I am often surprised by how many people think nursing home care is covered by Medicare, but this type of care is not. The government program that pays for nursing home care is called Medicaid, which is resource-based. As a general rule of thumb, your income must be below a certain level and assets must be below $2,000 excluding your primary residence before qualifying for Medicaid.

If your monthly exceeds the allowed amount, some states will allow for the establishment of a Qualified Income Trust (QIT), which is also known as a Miller Trust. The QIT requires that all sources of income be deposited into your personal account first and then transferred into your Trust. All of your bills, including the nursing home, are paid out of your Trust. You will receive a monthly nominal allowance of around $50 per month, but that is all. I guess the government doesn't assume that you will need much money since you are living in the nursing home.

As far as the Joneses go, they should have done several things differently. At first, they hired a non-medical agency to take on the tasks of screening and training workers, not to mention making sure they had the staff to meet their needs twenty-four hours a day, seven days a week. In an attempt to save money, the family then hired their own family care givers which can be a mistake.

If you hire your own caregivers, you are required to get a federal tax identification number and pay employment taxes for the caregivers. These caregivers are employees; you can't simply pay them an hourly rate. A local accountant may be able to handle these employment-related duties for a fee.

You should also consider some of the other risks, such as injuries to workers. Prior to hiring your own caregivers, contact your homeowner's insurance agent to make sure that you are protected if a caregiver is hurt on the job. Chances are that you won't be protected under the insurance and can subject yourself to employment related lawsuits should an injury occur. When you consider all the cost and risk associated with hiring your own care givers, you will soon realize that using a non-medical agency is the best solution.

Another caution is the transfer of assets in order to deplete assets when trying to qualify for government assistance. Most states have a five-year look-back period and can disallow assistance due to the transfer of assets. There is an annual limit per person that is not subject to a gift tax. In the case of transferring the home to a son and daughter, this is no guarantee that the house will still be protected from a Medicaid lien.

You should also keep in mind that your home can be transferred to family members upon death on a stepped-up basis for capital gains purposes. If the quit claim deed was for a nominal amount such as $1 prior to death, then when it is sold the capital gain will be the sales price minus the $1. The transfer of the home may also be subject to a gift tax, as the value exceeded the annual limits. Prior to making one of these transfers, I would strongly recommend that you talk to your accountant and attorney.

Henry should have applied for Medicaid assistance prior to him needing admission to the nursing home. There is a community spouse allowance that splits the family's assets in half based upon the date of application. Medicaid has also expanded their services to include Home and Community Based services to allow individuals to receive care at the most cost-effective setting. This includes care at home and some assisted-living facilities. While this may reduce Henry's options due to the ability to pay, it would have at least preserved assets for when Louis needs care.

There are other estate planning techniques, such as Trust, that can be used to protect assets that are beyond the scope of this book. Most of the techniques require application more than five years prior to your needing long-term care services in order to not violate the five-year look-back period. Please contact an attorney who specializes in estate planning for more information on these techniques.

Chapter 5: Golden Years

When I die I want my last words to be,

"I left a million dollars under the . . ."

Author Unknown

* * *

Bob and June Diamond were enjoying their golden years and were in their nineties. Both had medical issues, but considering their age, they were doing okay. When first reaching retirement age, they had visited their attorney to have their Wills prepared, including naming each other as their financial and health care POA. They had also named a contingent POA should the other predecease them or they were unable to perform the duties. In their minds, they had taken care of all of the important legal work and could get back to enjoying their retirement.

Having no children, they were able to spend money on pretty much anything they wanted. Bob loved sports and his den was filled with memorabilia. June loved jewelry, furs, and all things flashy. Combined, they had a lifetime of accumulated property.

Bob's health started to decline and he soon died. After his death, relatives looked after June. One side of the family became concerned with some of the expenditures incurred by June, such as dining out, that seemed excessive. June's health declined to the point that she could no longer make her own decisions. Soon it became evident that she would no longer be able stay at home and was placed in a nursing home.

The person who was listed as her designated power of attorney was uncomfortable making decisions on behalf of June. Due to the large extended family, he sought a non-family member conservator. Ideally, the court prefers family members to serve in this capacity, but due to strained family relationships, the court appointed me as a third-party conservator.

My first duty was to prepare a property management plan of all June's assets, income, and expected expenditures. Fortunately, Bob and June had managed their affairs well and they had some assets to pay for nursing home care. Since June would not be returning to her home, I made the decision and sought court approval to sell her personal property and home.

You learn a lot about someone when you start going through his or her belongings. Bob was an airplane pilot during WWII. June's picture from when they were dating back in the forties was still in his wallet. They had kept love letters they had written to each other during the war, which I found to be very special. While I never knew them from a social standpoint, I was impressed with their love for each other.

Bob and June also loved their family and churches. Bob's family was smaller and he was Presbyterian. June had a lot of extended family members and was Catholic. They kept every Christmas card, letter, etc. from their extended families. I guess not having children themselves led to the closeness of all the nieces, nephews, grandnieces, and grandnephews.

I mentioned that they also loved their churches. Bob had tithed to the Presbyterian and June to the Catholic Church as evidenced by their many statements, receipts, checks, etc. Interestingly enough, their Wills were different, and whichever one died last would result in their church receiving some of the excess distribution. As far as I could tell, this was the only thing they might have disagreed on.

So why am I including June and Bob's story in this book? Because they had so much stuff in their house, there has to be a better way. I found all of their tax returns, which was great, but I also found bills from over fifteen years ago for small purchases, such as electric bills, etc. Bob was an avid golfer who must have had over one thousand golf balls in his basement. June had at least one thousand articles of shoes, costume jewelry, etc. I am over-exaggerating to provide a point, but they had a lot of stuff!

As soon as I became June's conservator, I started receiving calls and e-mails from family members speculating what others had already taken from the house. Not having ever walked in their house, I didn't know what Bob and June owned. Some items were already secured in a safe with an inventory by a couple of the relatives at Bob's passing, which was great, but speculations were made that other items hadn't made it that far and had already been taken by family members.

Family members started telling me what Bob or June had promised them. I am sure that they Bob and June had indeed made some promises and had their preferences as to who would receive what. I had no way of knowing who was promised what unless it was in writing.

By this time, feelings had already been hurt and accusations made. All the family members that Bob and June loved so much were now at odds over personal property they had owned. I am sure this was not the way that Bob and June would have wanted it, just as I know this is not what you would want to happen to your family.

The good news is that all of this family turmoil could have been prevented had Bob and June clearly spelled out there desires, in writing, as to the disposition of personal property, care, and compensation (if any). These are the types of items that aren't covered in a most Wills that can tear any family apart.

Takeaways

Every one of us will accumulate a lot of things over our lifetimes, most of which aren't valuable. We can do our family a favor by downsizing and only keeping items that are necessary or have sentimental value. As long as you file a timely return, there is no reason to keep your tax returns over seven years. If you don't make enough money to file a tax return, please let your family members know that as well. Many families have searched for tax returns that don't exist.

It is also a good idea to ask your family what personal property item(s) they would want should something happen to you. What one person thinks is junk may be the most valued sentimental treasure to another. For example, when I was a child, I remember the wooden praying hands on my grandparents' coffee table. As I grew up, I measured my hands by placing them into the praying hands. It may sound trivial to some people, but that was the item I always remembered, and I wanted that item as a memory of my grandparents. There wasn't any value to the item to anyone except me. Long story short, the praying hands were chipped and weren't in the best shape, so someone discarded them. Regardless of the condition, I wish I had the praying hands to this day.

Believe it or not, your heirs probably will not fight over money, as it is easily dividable. What they will fight over is your personal property. There have been many noted lawsuits over family members fighting over personal property, which is an item that you own and there is only one of those items. Bob was an Army pilot during WWII and several family members wanted his military flight book. Multiple family members wanted the flight book, from his brother who served in the war with Bob, to a nephew who served in the military after being encouraged to do so by Bob. So who should receive the flight book? When you decide, please let me know.

If Bob had specified who should receive the flight book, then it is a non-issue. He might have done this, but he hadn't put it down in writing. Anything you promise someone is not enforceable unless it is in writing. The best way to do this is through an itemized Codicil as an attachment to your Will. This legal document allows you to add and change your Will without having to have the Will completely redone.

Don't assume as Bob and June did that once all of their legal paperwork is done, such as Wills, POAs, etc., then you have done all you need to do. At some point in your life, you need to start getting rid of all your stuff. Ask your family about what they might want and you might be surprised at what they value. If you don't, you will be placing the burden of having your family spend days sorting through it all not long after your death. If it is important to you, by all means keep it. Just make sure you determine who the item should go to when you pass and your entire family will be thankful.

Chapter 6: Blended Family

Danny walks into the clubhouse of his private country club and sees all of his old golfing buddies who inquire about his new marriage to an 18 year old bombshell.

"I know that you have money, but how in the world did you convince that bombshell to marry you?" one asked.

Danny replied, "I lied about my age. Instead of telling her I was 69, I told her I was 96."

Author Unknown

* * *

Paul and Theresa Newland married in their seventies after both of their spouses had passed away. Bob had one adult daughter from his previous marriage, and Theresa had two sons from her previous marriage. None of the children and grandchildren lived close, which was one of the factors that led to their marriage, as both were lonely after the loss of their lifelong companions.

Paul owned a construction business and had accumulated a significant amount of assets after the sale of his business. Theresa also had a fair amount of assets but nothing compared to Paul. They both sold their homes and bought a single-level home where they didn't have to worry about stairs. Then one day Paul passed away from a heart attack.

Both families were cordial and supportive of Theresa after Paul's death until Paul's daughter realized that a sizeable portion of her dad's assets now belonged to Theresa. The single-level home, the joint bank accounts, etc. were set up in such a way that they all belonged to the surviving spouse. Only a small life insurance policy and some investment accounts had the daughter listed as the beneficiary, but nothing else.

Paul's Will, on the other hand, listed his daughter as the sole heir to his assets. The daughter sought legal counsel and was given little hope of recourse. She was floored. A woman she hardly knew now owned most everything that her dad worked so hard to achieve over his lifetime. Needless to say, the daughter was not a happy camper and let everyone around her know it, especially Theresa.

As a footnote, it is my understanding that Theresa's Will leaves most everything to her two sons. Do you think Paul's daughter will be added to Theresa's Will after creating such a fuss? I don't think so.

Takeaways

I don't know if it was Paul's intent to leave most of his assets to his new wife Theresa or his daughter. More than likely it was his daughter. When buying the home and establishing bank accounts, he probably didn't even think about the ownership implications upon his death.

If you are unaware, the order of precedence is:
1) Property Titles
2) Beneficiary Designations
3) Trust
4) Wills

Most people think that the Will supersedes everything else, but it does not. Another common mistake is naming your estate as the beneficiary; this causes all kinds of tax implications when trying to liquidate individual retirement accounts (IRA) and other retirement accounts. It is always better to name an individual; just ask any investment advisor.

You also need to make sure that your desired beneficiary information is up to date. And while we are at it, you need to keep your life insurance policy(s) in a safety deposit box or other secure location. Did you know that over $1 billion in life insurance proceeds go unclaimed every year simply because no one knew that about the policy?

When you are in a blended family due to a second marriage because of a divorce or after the death of your first spouse, it is best to keep separate banking accounts. This provides some sense of security for your heirs that funds have not been comingled. In the case with Paul and Theresa, whichever side of the family died first, their heirs were going to lose. Since Paul died first, then the daughter lost part of her inheritance. Had Theresa died first, then the two sons would have lost out. This is not to say that the adult children were money vultures waiting for their parent to die (they were not), but it is rational to think that each parent would want their children to share in the inheritance.

I don't know the amount of assets Paul and Theresa each brought to the marriage. As stated above, it is my understanding that Paul brought considerably more than

Theresa. If that were the case, it may have been better for Paul to have purchased the home in his name only. This would have removed the property title conflict with the Will. Some sort of equalization of assets should be your approach to protect your heirs and reduce the potential for family conflict.

Trusts are also a great way to protect assets for your heirs and also supersede the Will. If money is held in a Trust, it is not considered a marital asset should the Trust beneficiary get a divorce. Trusts are beyond the scope of this book, so you should contact your attorney and make sure that you fully understand the advantages and disadvantages.

Conclusion

A pastor asked a lady if she had any dying wishes and the lady answered, "Yes. I want to be cremated and I want to have my ashes scattered across the local Walmart."

She continued, "Then I know that my daughter will come by and see me at least twice a week."

Author Unknown

* * *

As fate would have it, I had a client die while finishing this book. Sitting by his bedside, my thoughts once again raced as to what this client could tell me. Would he tell me about what it was like growing up as a child? Maybe it would be his fondest memories of holidays shared with family, or his teen years. I am sure he would share how he met his wife and how he loved his stepchildren even though he was unable to have any of his own. I wonder what it was like being a truck driver for a local company, and what changes he has experienced over his lifetime. All of these experiences just died.

In other cultures, seniors are revered for their wisdom. You have accumulated a lifetime of wisdom. There are things you wish you hadn't done or hadn't said. There are things you are glad you did and said. If you are still able to breathe and hold a pen, then your job is not yet finished. If I can encourage you to do anything in this book, it would be to *write down a personal message to each one of your family members*. This will be the lasting memory that they will cherish for the rest of their life. Trust me when I say that this will be the most prized possession you could ever give them.

By reading this book, you most likely have family and friends who will be by your side when you pass. You are loved and should consider yourself very fortunate. There are those who die every day who have no one by their side, and that is sad. I have provided a checklist for your use that summarizes the suggestions in this book. By completing it, you will have taken some major steps in protecting your family from some of the pitfalls that can tear it family apart.

In closing, I will share one other tidbit. One of the pillars of the church where I attended as a youth was named Noah. He was married to a wonderful Christian lady who preceded him in death. Noah loved to be around others and would often sit in the mall. The last time I saw him, I asked him how he was doing. His reply, "I am doing fine but I sure hope that God takes me to heaven soon." When I asked him why, he said "I just don't want my wife and family to think that I didn't make it."

Benjamin Franklin once said "Some people die at 25, they just aren't buried until 75." I hope and pray that you have many years to go until you die, and during that time you love, forgive, share, and prepare for the inevitable. May God richly bless you and put a hedge of protection around your family. Amen.

Step-By-Step Guide
(Professional Assistance Required)

Your family should have a listing of your attorney, investment adviser, accountant, and insurance agent. They should also know which funeral home you prefer to use.

Attorney (preferably one who specializes in estate planning)

1) Will
    a. May need to include language related to remarriage by spouse
    b. Pay close attention when blended families are involved

2) "Springing" general durable power of attorney(s)

3) Health care power of attorney(s)

4) Codicil—personal property listing

5) Trust, if warranted

Investment Advisor

1) Consultation as to the tax consequences, if any, to the investments held and what options provide the least tax consequence should you need to withdraw for long-term care expenses.

2) Confirm the beneficiary is your spouse and/or children (DO NOT list the estate as the beneficiary).

Accountant

1) Make sure all taxes filings are current.

2) Make sure your family knows if your income no longer requires you to file an income tax return.

Insurance Agent

1) Ensure up-to-date beneficiary information is listed.

2) Purchase long-term care insurance if possible. (Investment advisor may also sell these products).

3) Purchase a final expense policy, if warranted.

Funeral Home

Schedule an appointment with your funeral home of choice to:

1) Purchase pre-need burial policy (preferred over final expense policy).

2) Select casket, plot, headstone, etc.

The following items are ones that you and your spouse will need to complete.

Care giving

1) Develop an Advanced Medical Directive (AMD) such as the suggested 5 Wishes; clearly establish what treatment you want and don't want to include when food and water should be withheld.

2) Discuss your AMD desires with your health care power of attorney to make sure they fully understand your wishes and that *they are able to fulfill them.*

3) If living alone, consider a home alert system to where you can get assistance at the push of a button (I suggest ones that include a lockbox with a key for your front door so that emergency personnel can get to you without having to break down a locked door).

4) Determine whether family caregivers should be compensated, and if so, how much. Some long-term care insurance policies will pay for care given by family members. Check your policy for details.

5) Before having an outside caregiver provide care, secure all valuables in a safety deposit box.

Personal Property

1) Develop a list of valuable items as to who should receive what at your passing, sign, and date. This can be included as a codicil to your will and updated on occasion.

2) Ask family members what they might want. Don't throw out items you might think are junk.

3) Throw out all items that are not necessary, especially old bills, checks, etc.

4) Take unwanted clothes, furniture, etc. to organizations that can give them to the needy.

5) Remember that the spoken word dies when you do. Put your wishes down in writing whether it is in permanent ink on the item or on paper.

Safety Deposit Box

At a minimum, the following items should be included in your safety deposit box:

1) Birth certificates

2) Marriage license

3) Death certificate (if spouse predeceases you)

4) All legal documents other than the health care power of attorney and advanced medical

directive, which should be maintained at your residence

5) Investment insurance policies

6) Personal property listing

7) Car, boat, RV, etc., as well as titles

8) Anything of value that can easily be converted to cash

9) Letters to your loved ones! (The most prized memory you can ever give your loved ones)

Helpful Links

American Bar Association – Estate Planning Info & FAQs
www.americanbar.org/groups/real_property_trust_estate/resources/estate_planning.html

Five Wishes - AMD   www.agingwithdignity.org

Long-term Care Information   www.longtermcare.gov

Medicaid   www.healthcare.gov/medicaid-chip

Medicare   www.medicare.gov

MetLife – Broken Trust: Elders, Family & Finances Article
www.metlife.com/assets/cao/mmi/publications/studies/mmi-study-broken-trust-elders-family-finances.pdf

National Guardianship Association   www.guardianship.org

Society of Certified Senior Advisors   www.csa.us

Social Security   www.ssa.org

Veterans Administration   www.va.gov